DISCOURAGEMENT DOUBT & COMPROMISE

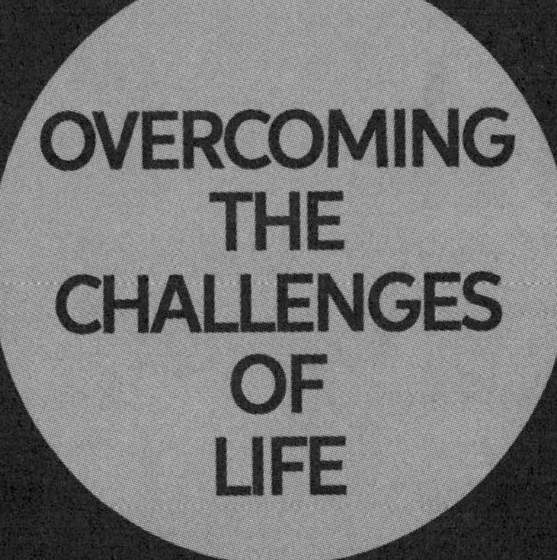

PASTOR RAY HADJSTYLIANOS

Discouragement, Doubt, & Compromise
– Overcoming the Challenges of Life

Published by Book Ripple Publishing
www.BookRipple.com

ISBN: 978-1-951797-06-5
Printed in the United States of America

To order go to:
www.PastorRayNY.com

"For I, the Lord
your God, will hold
your right hand,
saying to you, 'Fear
not, I will help you.'"
(Isaiah 41:13)

PREFACE TO OVERCOMERS

You are an overcomer. You were born to be an overcomer. That is how you were created and how you were programmed by God.

Why is that the case?

As a Christian, God has a plan, a purpose, and a destiny in store for you, but for you to accomplish it all, you will need to overcome anything and everything that gets in your way.

To accomplish God's plan, to achieve your purpose, and to reach your destiny, you will need to accept your role as that of an overcomer.

Be confident that your destiny awaits!

You are an overcomer. That is a fact you need to be reminded of, constantly, no matter how young or how old you might be or how long you've been a Christian.

Not only is it a fact, an encouraging outlook on life and a powerful belief – it is also the truth. Let that settle down deep in your heart, soul, and spirit.

In all that God has planned for you, it is His wish and desire that it come to pass, but it will require that you first overcome. Sure, it will take some faith and work, but it will all be worth the effort!

But you must first become an overcomer and more than a conqueror.

May the words you are about to read encourage and equip you in your journey to overcome!

– Pastor Ray Hadjstylianos

Table of Contents

Introduction to Overcomers

You were created with a destiny and a purpose. God has great plans for you.

What is more, Jesus clearly stated that He is on your side:

> "I have come that they may have life, and that they may have it more abundantly." (John 10:10b)

Abundant life! Achieving your God-given potential! All with God's unlimited love and grace for you!

Wow, that is amazing ... and yet in this world we will have opposition. Your incredible destiny will not simply fall into your lap. It may not be easy but you have to take hold of it by:

- walking by Faith
- heeding the Word
- praying the Word
- believing in God
- holding steadfast to your faith in God

- trusting in Him
- standing firm
- pressing in
- patiently enduring
- doing everything necessary to always move forward

Yes, it will take effort on your part, but you can do it! Tending a garden is hard work, but the harvest comes, does it not? That principle applies to virtually every undertaking, and the diligence and effort required is all part of being an overcomer.

It is the law of sowing and reaping:

> "Do not be deceived, God is not mocked; for whatever a man sows, that he will also reap." (Galatians 6:7)

This spiritual principle always works, and it is designed to always work in your favor – if you do things God's way.

But there is something else that you as an overcomer need to know. You have an enemy, a very real enemy, who hates to see you achieve anything that God has for you.

Satan is that very real enemy who, ever since he was cast out of Heaven, has been doing his utmost to rob and steal from you. In the beginning he messed with Adam and Eve and today he tries to mess continually with you and me.

> "The thief does not come except to steal, and to kill, and to destroy. I have come that they may have life, and that they may have *it* more abundantly." (John 10:10)

He foolishly even tried to mess with Jesus, but that did not go so well, as we will soon discuss.

Realistically, being an overcomer means that you will have to contend with Satan, his devious henchmen, and his constant tricks, plots, and schemes to distract you, pull you away, knock you down, puff you up, knock you off track, or tempt you to quit.

But remember, Jesus is adamantly intent on you having an "abundant" life. In His Word, He told us so:

> "You are of God, little children, and have overcome them, because He who is in you is greater than he who is in the world." (I John 4:4)

You have Jesus, the Creator of the universe, the sacrificial Lamb, the One who brought forgiveness to the world, the King of Kings, and the Lord of Lords, living inside of you. Clearly, without question, greater is Jesus who is in you than Satan, who is in this world!

But still, the devil will fight fiercely against you anyway, because he is so deceived.

Two thousand years ago, after Jesus was baptized and led by the Spirit into the desert, the devil was there to tempt even Him.

In fact, he tempted Jesus for 40 days straight!

As you know, the enemy's plans were foiled. His tactics and best efforts were reduced to rubble. Jesus was tempted, yet did not sin. There was no discussion and no debate. He overcame by simply quoting His Father's Word, and so can you!

In the following pages, you will see the great plans God has for you: His unstoppable passion for you and His loving desire that you be the overcomer you were meant to be.

Yes, you were made to be an overcomer.

Chapter One

Discouragement's Trap

Years ago, I heard it said, "Discouragement is the greatest tool the devil has against God's people."

It reminded me of how many times I had been hurt by discouragement. It had a vicious way of trying to slow me down, make me doubt myself, put me in neutral, and make me want to quit.

It is indeed a powerful tool of the enemy. He uses it all the time and in every circumstance. And if discouragement is indeed his greatest tool, then I knew I had to know more about it so I would be better prepared to stand against it.

What I discovered along the way really opened my eyes. I could see just how effective discouragement can be in hurting people, destroying vision, and undermining destiny.

But I also discovered something else that gave me great hope in my battle against it:

> **"The chains of discouragement can only be as strong as their weakest link."**

That means you and me, every single one of us, can break free of discouragement. We can be free by breaking that weakest link!

When we see discouragement creeping into our lives, no longer can we be duped; no longer will we believe that lie; and no longer will we allow discouragement to have any power over our destiny.

Discouragement's Trap

Like the magician's sleight of hand, where you fail to see what is taking place right in front of you, likewise, discouragement is just an evil magician's trick that seeks to deceive and to trap you.

With discouragement, where you begin is not where you end up. The final results, if you were to see them in advance, would be so repulsive that you would immediately walk away.

But discouragement is tricky. It pulls you in. It can devastate your life, put you in prison, and trap you ... and you'll never see it coming!

The trap is a simple three-step plan that works against you 24 hours a day, 7 days a week, 365 days a year. It is a non-stop trick constantly being played against you!

To lift the curtain and to see this incredibly effective device of the enemy for what it really is, we must delve deeper and take a more detailed look at the three stages of discouragement.

Stages of Discouragement

When I was a young teenager, I heard about selling Christmas cards and winning fabulous prizes. I ordered the gift catalog and when it arrived, I flipped to the back of the catalog where the big prizes were listed. I saw what I wanted. It was a shiny, beautiful Schwinn bicycle and it could be mine! It was the best prize in the catalog!

> Discouragement is the ultimate Venus fly trap.

All I had to do was sell a bunch of Christmas cards. Surely, I could do that!

I planned to offer the cards to my family and then go door-to-door to all my friends in the neighborhood. I was pumped up. I was excited about that bike I was going to win.

By the end of the first day of selling, I was already discouraged. It was not going to be as easy as I thought. I had sold very few cards. My family was only marginally interested and most of my sure-thing neighbors politely declined.

Trudging home, disheartened, I began to doubt whether I could do it at all. Did I have what it took? Was I good enough? How long would it take? Doubt took root and began to grow.

Soon my enthusiasm and courage started to wane. By that evening, I was no longer so confident. In fact, I doubted I could even do it. I felt lousy.

Flipping to the front of the catalog where the smaller gifts were, I found something that I liked but didn't love – a small camera. It was not nearly as amazing as the Schwinn bicycle, but it was something I could earn based on the sales I had made.

What had happened? I became discouraged, I doubted I could do it, and I compromised what I really wanted. In my mind, instead of the bicycle, I settled for that small camera.

"That's normal," you might say. "It happens all the time."

Yes, it really is normal and it does happen all the time. You are right. There is nothing so amazing and unusual about my teenage sales flop. Not everyone can be a super-salesman!

What I did not know was that I had fallen right into that trap that always begins with discouragement. Years later, I realized my own sad tale was simply all about that evil magician's slight-of-hand that always starts with discouragement. For me, it went like this:

> **Stage#1—Discouragement.** I was sad, disappointed, partially shocked, and all-around disillusioned about not being able to sell those Christmas cards.
>
> **Stage#2—Doubt.** Based on the discouragement I experienced, I began to look at my situation and doubt my abilities. Did I have the skills to win the prize? I had decided not. No, not even close!
>
> **Stage#3—Compromise.** When I decided I did not have what it took, all courage and enthusiasm drained out of me. I willingly traded my big goal for a much smaller one. I compromised completely.

The discouragement cycle was complete and the trap sprung!

While the situations and the circumstances might change, this 3-fold plan of Satan never changes. It is always the same! He uses the same old tricks and hopes for the same old results: discouragement, doubt, and compromise.

Always remember, if he can first get you discouraged, you will soon start to doubt. And when doubt firmly plants itself in your spirit, his soothing bait of compromise cannot be far behind.

Discouragement, doubt, and **compromise** are the three dangerous stages every Christian must battle to avoid Satan's trap in order to live a righteous, prosperous, and meaningful life.

Discouragement's Plan

Everything begins at that doorway marked "discouragement." It is stage #1. But it is only a doorway, never the final destination.

It is vitally important you recognize that fact! We don't have to get discouraged and stay that way. Nobody has to stay discouraged all the time, but there is always something further that happens as a direct result of that initial discouragement.

Discouragement is quite simply the "doorway" that leads to doubt, and doubt leads to compromise. It is always a three-step process because your discouragement is only a part of the bigger plan. Discouragement never operates alone. It always has company.

But if you are discouraged and hang out long enough with those feelings and words, you will find yourself in that environment of doubt.

The discouragement led you there, whether you wanted to go there or not.

Discouragement is always a slippery slope. Once through that door, it can immediately lead you down toward that place of doubt.

> When you see the trick of discouragement for what it is, you will never be caught unaware again.

Unfortunately, when you are in that place, you begin to doubt everything: the call on your life, the promises of God you had always believed in, your abilities, and your future.

You may even begin to doubt God Himself!

Confusion runs rampant.

The enemy's plan is for you to keep sliding down and down until you splash into that stagnant pond called compromise.

It is there that you give up and settle for whatever you can get, which is never the best God had planned for you!

If there is to be any "give and take," it should be centered around this truth:

> **God gave it and we ought to take it. That means if God gave you a promise, then you can take it, keep it, and never give it up.**

But the devil's goal is NOT to only keep you discouraged. It is NOT only to keep you doubting. His one goal is to talk you OUT of the Lord's blessings! To get you to compromise!

Whenever you settle for something less than what the Father intended, you have compromised – and that is the biggest loss you could suffer!

If you are in a situation where compromise seems like the only option, ask yourself:

> "Am I falling for that old trick that starts with discouragement again?"

Next Time, See It Coming

Now that you know the end game – *that compromise is the desired end result of discouragement* – you should never be caught unaware again!

Of course, nobody sets out to compromise:

- Nobody wants to give in to another's demands.
- Nobody wants to make concessions.
- The very idea of compromise is crazy ... yet we do it all the time!

But that trick should no longer work. The curtain has been lifted because you now know how that game is played.

So the next time you find yourself at the door of discouragement, simply choose not to enter in.

Turn and walk away. Slam the door shut by immediately dealing with those words or thoughts of discouragement.

Discouragement crowbars its way into your heart to create a crack for doubts to seep in.

Rest assured, your heavenly Father does not work in doubt, discouragement, or compromise. He will continue to speak to you even as you are being bombarded by those things, but He will never subject you to them.

The Bible tells us "He is not the author of confusion." And while He simply doesn't work that way, remember that the enemy does!

Compromised, the Christian will always foolishly do or say one or all of the following:

- I'll take the path of least resistance.
- There is an easier way out.
- It's not worth the effort.
- The Lord just didn't show up.

Again, compromise is the enemy's goal and best weapon. He wants you to settle for anything less than what God intended for you.

Decide in your heart that you will not settle for anything less than the Lord's best for you.

You want exactly what He has for you.

And that means no compromise!

Now that you know a bit more about Satan's slight-of-hand regarding discouragement, it's time to stand tall and claim your prize!

That's what makes you an overcomer!

"For God is not the Author of confusion but of peace, as in all the churches of the Saints." (1 Cor. 14:33 NKJV)

CHAPTER TWO

DISCOURAGEMENT COMES TO US ALL

If you are in the pursuit of anything, especially the Lord's call on your life and the vision you have for your future, you will no doubt face discouragement. It happens to us all because discouragement is Satan's favorite tool and weapon of choice to use against us!

Sometimes the discouragement is fleeting – a momentary wall that you need to press through. Usually, however, it decides to set up shop and hang out for a while.

In my very early beginning days of ministry, I did not know how to handle discouragement. I would often feel helpless against it and sometimes that led to doubt. I might even doubt God's Word, doubt that my circumstances would change, and doubt pretty much everything.

If I stayed in that place long enough, I would have invariably ended up in compromise – perhaps even quitting the ministry and giving up my call, vision, hopes, and dreams.

We read in Scripture that the devil tried that very thing with Jesus in the desert. But Jesus was not weak. He would not get discouraged. He would not doubt His Father's Word, and He certainly would not compromise. The following is the recount of that event as told in the Gospel of Luke.

A Walk in the Desert

After Jesus was baptized and a voice from Heaven boomed, "... You are My beloved Son; in You I am well pleased" (Luke 3:22), He was led by the Holy Spirit into the wilderness. Such an extreme shift – from extreme mountain top experience to dry and alone in the desert!

After those 40 days of fasting, the devil, deceived as he is, knowing Jesus would be so hungry and thirsty and tired and alone that He, like other men, might be discouraged and doubting – and ready to compromise.

Three times, the devil twisted scripture in a brazen attempt to get Jesus to compromise, but Jesus was not discouraged! He was charged up!

Once again, Satan made that same fatal mistake that caused him to be cast out of Heaven. Once again, he convinced himself that he was better than God and was self-deceived enough to think that he could get the Son of God Himself, Jesus, to agree with him.

He even went so far as to offer Him all the earthly kingdoms that he now controlled: "If you will worship before me, all will be yours." (Luke 4:7 – NKJV)

What a victory it would have been for Satan to trip up Jesus and, as he tries to do to so many of us, trick Him into getting discouraged, falling into doubt, and eventually compromising.

> Decide in advance that you will not doubt the call of God in your life … ever!

How could Satan not know what a terrible error he was making in even trying to use the Word of God against Jesus, who actually is the Word?

Always remember, that although Satan is a cunning and powerful enemy and someone to always be on guard against, just as in his battle against Jesus, he is no match for you when you speak the Word of God!

And you do not have to be afraid of the devil, because you have power and authority over him. Yes, he is crafty, yet he is already defeated. Just as Jesus defeated him with the Word, so can you!

The devil's lies and tricks certainly did not work on Jesus, but that does not stop him from bombarding us with similar lies that might lead us to discouragement, doubt, and eventually compromise – Satan's favorite prize!

Yes, sometimes the journey is difficult, but just because it is difficult does not mean God is not in it or you will not reach your intended destination!

Just like Jesus, you do not need to compromise! But you must choose to stay on course – deal with the discouragements and doubts when they come, and you will reach the destination you desire.

Expect Discouragement to Come

Along the way, even on a daily basis, you can expect discouragement to come knocking.

It always does, no matter who you are or what you do.

Stay alert. Guard your emotions, your will, and your mind. That is where discouragement is going to try to grab hold, then burrow in and plant itself until you choose to compromise.

That is exactly what happened to the children of Israel as they were being led out of the land of Egypt. They had just witnessed a miraculous deliverance, which included walking right through the Red Sea on totally dry ground. But along the way, despite the miracles, the people began to get discouraged.

It was not long before they began to doubt. They grumbled:

> And the people spoke against God and against Moses: "Why have you brought us up out of Egypt to die in the wilderness? For *there is* no food and no water, and our soul loathes this worthless bread." (Numbers 21:5)

They began to curse their blessings. The people spoke against the Father and His leader, Moses, and demanded to know why they had been brought to the desert to die.

But God never said that! That was not His plan. He did not promise that they would die! In their doubt, they questioned Jehovah's real promises.

All they had to do was keep on walking and God would take them to a very good place! No, the journey was not promised to be easy, but He did promise that He would bring them into the Promised Land!

But discouragement and doubt had set in. They wanted to go back to Egypt rather than go forward into what God had for them. They were willing to compromise everything because they were hungry, tired, hot, thirsty, and sick of the manna bread from Heaven – the very bread that kept them alive!

Here's a thought that may seem trivial at first glance, but it is true and may be exactly what you need to hear:

> You may not yet have all you want or all the Lord intended, but don't curse what you do have. Don't doubt it. Your paycheck may not be the best, but don't curse it. Give the Father thanks and praise and keep going forward!

Moses, because he was such a great man of God, was able to rally the troops. He kept them marching, but they were discouraged. They doubted that God was even with them. They saw only their difficulties because they focused on their situation so much that they could not see the

Father's provision, protection, power, or love. All they saw were their problems.

Stop looking at your difficulties. Focus instead on Him, His Word, and Jesus. Difficulties will always be there, but Jesus, the Father, and the Holy Spirit are unchangeable. They will always be there too – much longer than any problem will ever be. They are steady. Their Word is sure. And the Word will always work in your life if you will put the Word to work.

> We all face discouragement … but we must confront and deal with it!

Read your Bible; believe what it says; act on what you've learned from it. The results will amaze you!

The children of Israel quickly forgot all that God had done for them ... and we do the very same thing! We forget where He has taken us. We forget the evident Hand of the Lord in our lives.

Discouragement hits and we doubt our Creator? We doubt His Word? "I can't do this anymore. He doesn't love me. I quit," people may say.

After all He has done for us, we get tripped up in discouragement, fall into doubt, and run right into Satan's trap and fully-blown compromise!

The truth is that the same strategy of discouragement, doubt, and compromise is thrown at each one of us in every area of life. You name it and most likely, it has happened.

This age-old trick will be thrown at you time and time again, but you must be on your guard against it. Expect it. And when you see it coming, you will know how to handle it.

Keep Going Forward

If you have a car accident, you don't throw away your keys and vow to never drive a car again, do you? If you get a speeding ticket or get stuck in traffic, you don't give up on the whole idea of driving, do you?

No, of course not! That would be silly. You keep on going. You get back in the car and you keep on driving. Maybe you are more careful and hopefully you are a better driver. Maybe you'll end up driving even a newer car!

But quitting would admittedly not be an option.

But in life's journey, the rules are for some reason different. People get weary and tired, discouraged and full of doubt, and they willingly compromise about all the good things they once did, wanted, and believed God would provide.

Why is that? Is it not just as silly, and even more so, to abandon a vision or goal or calling from Heaven because of circumstances along the way?

Compromise is usually the path of least resistance, which always appears to be much easier than stretching and learning and growing with God. But the route of compromise is also the route that will cost you the most. To compromise is to lose. That will always be the case.

God will settle it for you if you refuse to quit.

Instead of quitting, be committed to your own journey. Press through. Press on. No matter what the obstacle and no matter who may come against you, keep on going forward!

Yes, people will at times try to attack your integrity, values, rights, authority, and much more. But so what – God is with you!

There is something else you need to be on the lookout for.

As you trust God to take you where He wants to take you, don't be surprised when He does a new thing in your life.

And as you press forward, keep an eye out for the unexpected! Isaiah reminds us:

> "I will bring the blind by a way they did not know; I will lead them in paths they have not known. I will make darkness light before them, and crooked places straight. These things I will do for them, and not forsake them." (Isaiah 42:16)

It may be strange, new, illogical, and not entirely normal, but the Lord has many ways to bless you and to promote you.

Every step of the way, He will open doors of opportunity and make the seemingly impossible, now possible. And in addition, He promises never to leave you.

That is His commitment to you. That commitment will go a long way in calming the discouraging feelings, silencing the nagging doubts, and avoiding that disastrous compromise!

We All Face Discouragement

Discouragement is an experience that we all go through. Everyone faces it. There are no exceptions. It knocks on everyone's heart and mind. We all have to do battle with it at one time or another.

Admittedly, discouragement is one of Satan's most successful weapons, as is evidenced by how well it works. Spend a little time in discouragement and it is amazing how soon we begin to doubt the very things we have never before even vaguely questioned.

Yes, we all face it, but that does not mean we need to give into it!

Discouragement is not the destination but rather a slightly-ajar door that, unfortunately, can often lead us right to doubt and compromise.

> Only people in pursuit of a dream, vision, purpose, destination, or goal will be tempted at the door of discouragement!

And "compromise" is the devil's most desirous result – the very place where we quit, give up, and even turn back and run!

Close that door of discouragement. Slam it shut and walk away!

You do not need to go through that door at all. The best way to avoid the snare of discouragement is to deal with it as soon as it raises its ugly head!

Feeling less confident, less motivated, and less optimistic are signs of what discouragement looks like. Resist it. If not, and you walk through that door – the next step will be doubt.

Feeling hesitant, untrusting, uncertain, and insecure? That is what doubt feels like. Fight it. Hold fast to what you know to be true. Climb back up and out and slam the door behind you!

Personally, I have seen many get caught and trip on that doorway of discouragement. After first falling headlong into doubt, it is not long before they start compromising in one or many areas of their life.

Remember, there should never be discussion with the enemy. There is no arguing with the "facts" in the land of compromise. If God's Word is the truth and if He said it, then it is good enough and there is no further discussion necessary!

You can believe it and you can take it to the bank!

So, how best to fight discouragement, doubt, and ultimately compromise? Start by clinging tightly to the life-changing truths found only in the Holy Bible.

The Holy Spirit will help you navigate your way back out – past doubt and beyond the door of discouragement. Once closed, you will never need to go that way again!

Walk forward in faith, just as Scripture says:

> "So then faith comes by hearing, and hearing by the word of God." (Romans 10:17)

Faith comes by hearing the truth again and again. So walk by faith. Trust in God. And keep pursuing what you believe He has said He has in store for you.

What you are seeking, what you are believing for, and what you are desiring with all your heart will be yours. God will make sure of it.

That you can believe and count on!

It is amazing
what can
happen
when we
refuse to be
deterred!

Chapter Three

When the Journey Is Hard

Of all the reasons for discouragement and people giving up on their vision, dreams, goals, and the call on their lives, none is more common than the simple truth that **sometimes the journey through life can be difficult!**

But who said life would be easy? Who told you that your faith walk would be a cake walk? Who sold you that overly simplified fact?

For some reason, most of us expect more "tiptoeing through the tulips" than "slogging through the mud." We think life will be easy and are genuinely shocked when it is not.

But why do we think that way? Where does that untruth even come from?

Rather than painting a rosy picture of a life of ease and problem-free living, it would be far more beneficial and productive to say:

> "If you just stay committed to the journey and walk it out, then you will find yourself at the other side more blessed than when you started."

Yes, life is an adventure. And yes, it is hard work. But God is with you and it is promised that you will win in the end – if you stay connected to Him, connected to His Word, and committed to never giving up!

Created to Fly

You may have heard the story of the young boy who found a butterfly struggling to get out of its cocoon. He saw the stretching, pulling, and struggling of the small butterfly. He watched as it struggled to tear free, then collapsed inside the transparent wall, utterly exhausted by the effort. Then it would try again a few minutes later.

Trying to help, the boy carefully cut open the cocoon with his pocketknife. The butterfly was free!

He watched in delight as the butterfly flapped into the air. Then, suddenly, the butterfly dropped to the ground! It flopped around on the leaves for a few minutes, tried to steady itself, and then tipped over on its side and slowly died.

The boy sat there the whole time, coaxing the butterfly to get back up. "What's wrong?" he asked. "I helped you. I gave you an easier way out."

What the boy did not know was that in the natural struggle to break free from the cocoon, the butterfly was strengthening its tiny muscles so that it would have the ability to fly when the time came.

Without sufficient strength, the butterfly would never make it. The easy way out, in this case, proved to be fatal.

The plan and destiny for the butterfly was that it would fly. It was created to fly. But to achieve that destiny, it had to go through a hard, strengthening process full of exhaustive effort and struggle. Hard ... but necessary!

You were created to fly, too. Sometimes the journey may seem difficult, but those same difficulties are actually strengthening your faith muscles so that you can do what you have been created to do.

Burn this truth into your heart and mind:

> **"Just because the journey gets difficult does not mean God is not in it. In fact, in the most difficult times, He is in the**

middle of it all and leading you gently through it all."

Looking back on my life, in all the difficult times, I thought I had a much faster route, an easier route, for God to give me. But the Lord – *in His wisdom, mercy, and love* – allowed me to go the long way, the more difficult way, so that I would be ready and prepared for the next level of growth and success. I had to strengthen my faith muscles.

That is precisely what the Master does for you, for me, and for everyone who will let Him direct their lives. As a result of the learning and strengthening, you are able to achieve what it is you are seeking – and what God has planned for you.

The Task Is Often Hard

Usually the task is difficult. If it were easy, it would not be a task at all!

Nehemiah of the Old Testament understood that. He had a big vision and a very hard task. The walls of Jerusalem had been broken down and he had taken it upon himself to rebuild them.

Back in those days, walls meant protection for a city. Without walls, an enemy could easily attack, kill the inhabitants, and steal everything of value.

As soon as Nehemiah started the rebuilding, several leaders rose up to oppose him. Words were spoken and threats were made. The work itself was certainly difficult.

> Then Judah said, "The strength of the laborers is failing, and *there is* so much rubbish that we are not able to build the wall." (Nehemiah 4:10)

Discouragement was knocking, loudly! But Nehemiah was smart. He was also a great leader. He instructed the people to build with a tool in one hand and a sword in the other!

> You have the capacity and the ability to do the impossible.

The lies, the angry threats, and the pressure from the opposition did not have its intended effect on his workers.

They refused to get discouraged. Nehemiah knew exactly how that trick of the enemy worked, and he led the people away from that open doorway of discouragement.

As a result, they accomplished the impossible, and did so in a mere 52 days!

Yes, the task was hard. It was dangerous, even life-threatening, but Nehemiah and all the workers stayed on course. They looked to Jehovah for strength and kept moving forward.

Just as with Nehemiah, it is amazing what can happen when we refuse to be discouraged about the difficulties surrounding the purpose God has for us. Whatever it is we are aiming for, it is possible to achieve, if we keep at it.

Literally, there is no task that cannot be accomplished! You have the power and wisdom and ability from God Himself. Tasks are often bigger than what you may think you can do, but our Father has bigger plans and He can help make the "impossible" possible.

Shake Off Discouragement

Pause for a moment and think about these questions:

> Have you ever had to face discouragement head-on? Even when you were sure God was behind your efforts?

No doubt you did. It is completely normal. Everyone does.

> How many times in your life have you been discouraged, doubted, and then fallen into compromise?
>
> Did you see later what you missed out on by making that compromise?

Sometimes in our perfect 20/20 rearview mirror hindsight, what we missed and could have had can be the most agonizing part of all. We know what could have happened and what was supposed to happen, yet we missed it because we fell for Satan's old trick of discouragement.

If I'm describing you, do not be discouraged all over again. Don't feel guilty! Instead, this time around, whatever it is you are pursuing, know that the Holy Spirit can strengthen you and enable you to press through to reach your goal.

This time, you are not going to let discouragement lead to doubt – and doubt lead to compromise. There will be no compromise. This time you will win! This time the trick of the enemy will not work.

Know without doubt that this is His divine plan for you. This time is your time! No more compromise! Stick to your guns! Deal with discouragement when it comes up.

Do not settle for anything but the dream you are chasing.

Why Hard May Often Be Good

The butterfly is a great example of why difficulties can be good. For our butterfly, the struggle and effort would have produced strength, which is a prerequisite to flying and life itself.

In your life, you learn, you grow, and you mature. You will see you are stronger than you thought. It is here that the Creator proves who He is in your life!

People naturally want things easy and fast, but tomorrow could be the day of your breakthrough. If you get impatient and quit today, you could miss that – and maybe your destiny!

Anything worth having is worth fighting for.

Nobody knows the future, but you can rest assured that your Father in Heaven does and is directing your steps. He is with you. But, He wants you to trust Him and believe in Him.

Even if it is hard going, He is there with you. He is going to show Himself mighty

… and He will turn your situation into something good!

In the heat of the moment, it is vital to keep the proper perspective. Always remember:

Keep the Good Perspective … Avoid the Traps!

You know that if discouragement festers, it can only lead to doubt, and from there you are on a straight path to compromise. But you know this trick of the enemy and how it works.

Keep the proper perspective by always being on guard for his tricks. Instead of letting discouragement build itself up, knock it down right away with the power of the Word of God! Pump up your own tires! And without doubt, it always helps to keep the door of discouragement tightly closed.

The next time you are faced with some difficulty, reject the temptation to get discouraged. Throw out any thoughts of doubt. You already know what Satan's game plan is.

If you see discouragement coming, you know that doubt and compromise cannot be far behind. Call the enemy's bluff and walk away.

Keep the Perspective ... Walk On!

To get where you want to go, you must press on. But a bumpy road, a rough patch, a challenging time, a setback of your dream, or not seeing what you expected to see, is hard to get past. Do not let yourself get discouraged. Keep the right perspective and walk on!

> Faith works if you will work your faith.

The goal of the enemy is to get you to compromise, but if you refuse to get off track or let discouragement get a hold in your life, you will never compromise but will eventually achieve your goal.

Yes, sometimes that means trusting when you cannot see your own hand in front of your face! But do it. Keep at it. Commit to the journey. That is an expression of your faith. Again, always remember:

> "For we walk by faith, not by sight." (2 Corinthians 5:7)

Walking by faith rather than by sight is, of course, not always going to be easy, but you know you will win if you keep at it, persist, and stay focused.

One of the reasons the journey feels so "hard" is because God usually has bigger plans for you than you do for yourself. This is more true than most of us like to admit.

Trust Him to bring it to pass as you doggedly hang on and stay committed to the task.

You will eventually reach your destination.

Just walk on! That is the right perspective in the middle of challenging times.

Keep the Perspective ... You'll Be Better For It!

Sometimes the job is difficult. If the task is bigger than you expected, and you hang in there and press forward, you are going to be better for it.

As you are stretched, your faith and abilities stretch too! You become stronger as you walk in a whole new level of trust with the Almighty One!

Difficult situations can perfect your faith. You learn at your core how to trust and believe in God, and that matures you at a rate faster than you could have hoped for.

Most people bail out when the going gets tough. Whatever the scenario – whether it is relationships or work or college or business or marriage or parenting – or even church – people would rather walk away than deal with whatever is difficult.

What they don't realize is that by choosing to walk away, they are choosing to remain weak. If they had only stuck with it, they would have become stronger, smarter, more successful, and not compromised, just like that butterfly!

Walking away fixes nothing! In fact, it makes things worse, and remaining weak is no way to face your tomorrows.

Just because the going is hard does not mean you will not win! Remain committed to the journey and you will win. By doing so, you prove your faith, you strengthen your muscles, and you are ready to do even greater things!

Truly, battling the hard things is good.

Your Testimony

When you have walked it out, fought the good fight, stood your ground, and have seen your vision or dream come to pass, you have a testimony! That is power. It is living proof that God did in your life exactly what He said He would do. It is proof that faith and God's Word work.

And that is precisely what the enemy does not want you to have. He does not want you to finish a race because the end result of finishing your race is glory to God, growth in your own life, and a rock-solid testimony that encourages others.

Do you know what that means for you?

> "And they overcame him by the blood of the Lamb and by the word of their testimony ...." (Revelation 12:11a)

Your testimony is the proof. People are not impressed with what you say or even the fact that you are walking by faith. However, they cannot argue with your testimony. It is proof. Your testimony is undeniable evidence.

That is precisely why, in all you attempt to accomplish, the enemy tries to get you to compromise. In so doing, he neutralizes you and leaves you with no testimony at all.

So the next time you see the door of discouragement cracked open, even just a little bit, slam it closed with a vengeance! And the next time you are tempted to quit, challenge yourself to stay committed to the journey.

Discouragement cannot lure you through the doorway if you are too busy chasing the calling and dreams that you have! If you want it, and it is worth having, then it is worthy staying on course and on the journey.

> Close the door on discouragement! If you don't get what you want, maybe that's God's way of protecting you.

Quit or compromise?

Not a chance!

Press forward. Stay the course. Then you will, just as God intended all along, benefit from His promises in your life. He wants you to receive the rewards of pressing through. He wants you to have the proof. He wants you to have the breakthrough. He wants you to have a testimony!

He wants you to win!

Chapter Four

When It Appears Others Got My Blessing

Many years ago, when our little church had only 150 people and $150,000 in the bank, I felt God was challenging us to proceed with the new church building project anyway, despite those limitations.

Feeling strongly that the Lord was calling us to do it, I boldly proclaimed that we were going to move forward in faith. God would provide! I told our small church family that He would make it happen. Just have faith for the miraculous.

Halfway through the building project, I was standing in the middle of the unfinished church sanctuary, sadly considering our situation. We were 50% complete, but we were 100% out of money – and every bank refused to loan us any more!

Admittedly, I was feeling a little discouraged. Would we survive? Was my reputation on the line?

In the middle of all this, a staff member hit me with some startling news. A church down the road had just received a million-dollar donation from some wealthy businessman!

My immediate reaction was, "That businessman went to the wrong church! What's more, that church is not even in a building project!"

It didn't make sense. I was in disbelief. I was envious and for a brief moment in time, I was even more discouraged! But I then did what I knew to be right and got on my knees and prayed in a halting voice, "God, bless that church. Thank you for blessing them."

Achievements and prosperity of others should not get you down. It should get you up!

No, I did not feel like praying that prayer, but it was the right thing to do. It was the right thing to say and to pray. It was my way of slamming shut the door of discouragement.

It certainly seemed like the other church had just received what I needed and was believing God for, but I chose to pray blessing over them and over our own building plans. It was my responsibility to keep at it. I knew that.

I could simply keep at it or let discouragement lead me to doubt and eventually compromise.

God Gets Ready to Do a Miracle

Thankfully, we prayed our way through the balance of the construction. Because of the faithfulness of the church family to give generously through offerings to our building fund, we slowly paid down our bills. This was certainly not as the result of anyone giving us a million dollars!

Eventually, the building was completed and we moved in. Attendance began to steadily increase and the memory of the miraculous million-dollar donor at the other church faded as we settled into the daily work of the Lord.

But while we had pretty much forgotten about the million-dollar miracle, our faithful God had not!

He remembered my prayer for financial favor. He remembered my prayer of thanksgiving for the blessings bestowed on that first Pastor who got the million dollars.

And, because the Bible clearly states that there is no prayer of the righteous that goes unanswered, God was getting ready to spring into action on our behalf. He was about to answer that prayer, but we had no clue of the tremendous miracle that was about to take place!

The Miracle

Several years after we opened the doors to our new church, a well-known, talented, and very wealthy professional athlete and his family joined our congregation. He and his wife and children quietly attended. They were a very humble family who sat in the back, always kind and attentive.

Despite his busy travel schedule with his team, they were faithfully involved in several ministries. They were not seeking any special recognition or favor, and to the best of my knowledge, gave only one larger-than-usual offering over and above their weekly tithe.

Those who knew him as a sports celebrity respected his privacy, and as his Pastor, I did the same. Actually, we had little more than a casual friendship until after they had been attending for about a year. It was then that he called me privately.

After thanking me for ministering to him and his family, he explained that he wanted to make our church his permanent church. Although his career kept him on the move, they had settled in our area for the time being and wanted to call our church "home."

He explained that as committed tithers, they had struggled with how to tithe because they were seldom in one church for very long. As a result, they had created a "tithe account" to hold their previous years' tithes until they had a home church to sow it into.

"We feel the Lord wants us to sow it here," he stated. "Can I have my accountant call you directly and arrange for the transfer of funds? I believe there's a little more than a million dollars in that account."

My jaw hit the floor. You can imagine my shock!

Several days later when he called to make the transfer, the accountant explained, "The actual amount in this tithe account, Pastor, is $1,300,000."

The Lord made the miracle even more spectacular! And He was not finished with us yet. One year later, that same accountant called to inform me there was additional money that needed to be transferred from that tithe account to our church. It was another $500,000!

There is no doubt in my mind:

> **Had I gotten a bad attitude and sour heart over that other pastor getting his million dollars and became envious, discouraged, jealous, doubtful, and compromised – *we would have totally missed our blessing!***

Instead, that first pastor and church received a million-dollar miracle, but we received a $1,800,000 miracle!

Why?

It's simple:

> "God does not show favor to one man more than another." (Romans 2:11 NLV)

> "But without faith it is impossible to please Him, for he who comes to God must believe that He is, and that He is a rewarder of those who diligently seek Him." (Hebrews 11:6 NKJV)

Proof of God's Goodness

Standing that day in that half-finished building with seemingly impossible odds against us, things did not look good. Not good at all! But what I saw with my eyes and what I knew in my brain was not the whole story because you never know what is right around the next corner!

You may be on Hardship Highway ... about to turn onto Blessing Boulevard! You could be only minutes, days, or weeks away from blessing or breakthrough. You just don't know!

What you do know is this:

> **You cannot let discouragement knock you out of the game. You cannot let doubt pull you down. Stay committed to the journey and your task and you will one day see it come to pass. You will bear fruit!**

In the meantime, rejoice with those who are rejoicing. Be happy for them. Do not get offended or angry or jealous of those who get what you are fighting so hard to achieve. Learn from them, if there is anything to learn, and know in your heart that your day is coming.

If God has said it and you are believing Him for it, then you can rest easy, knowing it will be yours. If God said it, that settles it, and that is reality. After all:

> "God is not a man, so He does not lie. He is not human, so He does not change His mind. Has He ever spoken and failed to act? Has He ever promised and not carried it through?" (Numbers 23:19 NLT)

Neither does He show favoritism. What He does for one person (the person who received the blessing you have been waiting for!) He will do for another. He will do it for you as well – if you will dare to believe Him, stand in faith, stay on course, and stand up against the discouragement.

When that miracle money came to our church, we were able to pay off our debts, eventually purchase another piece of property, and so much more. It was an incredible boost to our entire ministry.

> Your day of breakthrough is closer than it was yesterday!

It was the best we could expect, and more!

But it was also an incredible boost to my personal faith, our faith as a church body, and the faith of everyone to whom we told the story. It was proof of God working in our lives to bring about His will and His purposes!

Our church and our lives have never been the same. It was as if shock waves went out in every direction.

No wonder the enemy tries so hard to trap us with discouragement and doubt. He wants us to compromise and miss all those wonderful things that our Father has planned for us.

When Others Get What You Want

When you get what others have been longing for, do you want them to be discouraged because you got what they were praying for? Of course not! A dream fought for and a goal accomplished should be a cause of celebration for everyone.

Settle in your heart that your mind and emotions will do the obvious:

> **The advancements, prosperity, and achievements of others will encourage me to trust God all the more. If He does it for them, He will do it for me!**

The next time you see someone get what you have been looking for, praying for, and needing, smile and rejoice with them – even when you don't feel like it. Be happy for them. Keep your faith and trust in God that your day is coming.

Rejoicing with others will actually protect you, just as David proclaimed:

> "But as for me, my feet had almost stumbled; my steps had nearly slipped. For I was envious of the boastful, when I saw the prosperity of the wicked." (Psalms 73: 2-3)

Anytime you are envious, you set yourself up for a fall. Envy is never helpful. All it does is make you more discouraged – simply leading you more quickly into doubt and compromise.

Is There Enough to Go Around?

When you are watching others receive what you wanted, it is tempting to think, "It worked for them, but it's not working for me."

That sulking attitude will do you no good. In fact, entertaining a sour attitude is one of the quickest ways to open the door to discouragement. You don't want to do that!

When others get what you have wanted, it's tempting to think as I did, "That person received my blessing."

That's simply not the truth. True, the other person did receive a blessing, but it was *their* blessing, not yours. God has more than enough in store to meet the needs of everyone!

When others are blessed, it's tempting to question (like I did), "God, did you give the wrong thing to the wrong person?"

As if He could have actually made a mistake!

The Father did not mess up the addresses or mistakenly send your package to the wrong house! He has a plan and He never messes up any of the details, no matter how small and insignificant they might appear to you.

The best thing to do is to be happy for others. Rejoice with them. And keep on believing and trusting God for your miracle to come, too!

> "Rejoice with those who rejoice, and weep with those who weep." (Romans 12:15 NKJV)

After all, isn't He called "El Shaddai," the Sovereign God, the God who is "more than enough" for us?

There is more than enough in the Lord's Kingdom for you to have what you are believing and trusting Him to provide.

Because God moves so miraculously through other people, while He is working on the blessing you are asking for, He may also be working on the blessings someone else needs to bring your blessing to you.

And it's important to remember that often the goals, dreams, and desires of that person bringing your blessing may be fulfilled before yours.

So I encourage you therefore to be patient and simply:

- Relax.
- Remain committed to the journey.
- Give no room to envy.
- Rejoice with others.
- Maintain your faith.
- Trust that blessings will flow as you obey the Word of God.
- Hold on – your day of blessing and harvest is coming.

You may be just about ready to turn the corner. Do not allow any room for discouragement to establish a foothold. Drown any thoughts of doubt with

God's Word. Speak the truth and keep yourself encouraged.

Your day will come!

Delay is often on purpose because we are not ready for success.

CHAPTER FIVE

WHEN IT TAKES TOO LONG

Relevant to every goal is something over which we have little or no control.

Everyone understands it, yet it is elusive and very much a mystery.

We all have to respect it because it is so necessary, yet it is often despised.

We want badly to be able to control it, yet it is always absolutely out of our control!

It is the concept of "time" and everything is subject to it.

God's Word recognizes it and tells us how to best handle it:

> "And let us not grow weary while doing good, for in due season we shall reap if we do not lose heart." (Galatians 6:9 NKJV)

Apparently, there is an appointed time for everything, but while we wait for that appointed time, it may benefit us to consider:

- Trusting that the Father knows best and that He has our appointed time all figured out.
- Until the appointed time, spend days wisely in learning, growing, and working on your own personal development.

Most simply put, it usually takes a lot longer for a dream and vision to come to pass than we think it should.

Standing in the Middle

Could delay mean, we're simply not always prepared to handle the blessing God has waiting for us?

I have ministered to people who want desperately to run their own business, but in their everyday lives do they make $1 and spend $2?

Can they manage other people? Can they balance a budget? Do they have good people skills? Are they a person of character? If they rush things, do they achieve their goal only to quickly lose its benefits again?

If they can't run their own lives, how can they manage the complexities of a business?

Similarly, a lot of single people often want desperately to be married, but can they balance a checkbook? Do they have a nagging personality? Are they spoiled? Do they even know how to treat a mate? Do they have a job? Are they in debt?

Frustration or preparation … you get to choose.

So the time it may take to prepare for marriage might be a very good thing! Without adequate preparation, which always takes time, it's possible to destroy the very thing meant to be a blessing.

The journey through time can be a terrible time of **frustration** or a wonderful time of **preparation**.

It's your choice.

Use the time in the middle – the time between the goal and seeing that goal come to pass – to prepare.

Work on yourself during the delay window. Ask God what He wants to do in your life. What do you need to learn? What keys are missing?

Your Father does not want you to mess it up and fail. He has not made you to be a failure. He wants to bless you, and for you to be able to handle the blessing!

Patience during a time of preparation will help you fight discouragement. It will make you stronger. It will prepare you for the bright future to come.

We can't influence time in order to change it. Our job is to simply press forward.

And God has already given us the answer concerning patience and about how to best handle time:

> "Therefore be patient, brethren, until the coming of the Lord. See how the farmer waits for the precious fruit of the earth, waiting patiently for it until it receives the latter and the former rain. You also be patient. Establish your hearts, for the coming of the Lord is at hand." (James 5:7-8)

You stand the strongest by walking *in* Him and walking *with* Him. So keep on standing. Do not quit and you will see your goal and vision and desire come to pass.

When it does come, it will come quicker than you thought it would - and it will be better than you could have imagined!

Trust the Maker

Your dreams, visions, and plans are often very dependent on other people being in the right place and willing and submitted to God's purposes.

For example, if you are believing for a dream job, that opening must first be created by someone else leaving that job, which now makes that position available for you.

It shouldn't be a surprise then when God uses someone else, obedient to His prompting, to sow a blessing into your life.

This isn't a matter of coincidence, but rather a matter of the Lord's perfect timing!

No matter what the circumstances, it will take time for life's events to come together and time for our Creator to get all the pieces in the right places!

Sometimes it is difficult for us to trust in God's timing, but remembering that God has His own timetable: trust the Maker, stand in faith, continue to declare the vicory, and walk in patience and love.

It will all soon come together!

The Process Brings Perfection

In His divine process, God molds, changes, and develops you from an insufficient, insecure, weak person into a mature, strong, God-trusting individual. That is what He wants to do for each one of us. That is His plan.

What you become as a result of His working in your life is exactly what the devil wants you to miss. He wants you to fail, to be pulled off target, so you are not transformed but rather compromised.

Never forget that God cares about you.

But don't focus on the timing or delays. Don't believe you are stuck and not moving forward or that you cannot handle God's schedule. Instead, keep your eyes on the Lord and on your dreams and your progress.

And don't allow yourself to get distracted by the timing. Let the Lord handle that part. After all, it's His schedule, His way. You cannot impose your time table onto the things of the Creator.

Stay with it. You will eventually arrive. Remember, He always knows the exact time of your arrival!

Personally, there have been many times when I wanted to have things done according to my schedule. That brought me nothing but discouragement and frustration.

I found out that Jesus does not need our help. He can get us to where we need to be at the right time. No, it is not necessarily my timetable, and often the road may be bumpy, but eventually I do get to where I need to be.

It is His schedule, and I am better off for following it.

Can You Control Your Timing?

When I started our church many years ago, several people said, "You'll have 500 people within 12 months!"

Though it was flattering to hear and it was something I wanted to hear, reality was another matter. We had maybe 50 people at the end of that first year.

Of course I wanted a quicker way, an easier way! It felt like we were going the difficult way, the slow way, and I wanted desperately to find a faster way to my goal.

The truth for me, and for you, is that if we take a shortcut, we will likely not be ready for the end result. We will not be able to handle our success if we achieved it via a shortcut!

Timing is often a distraction.

The Children of Israel could have taken a shortcut from Egypt to the Promised Land. Jehovah could have taken them through a shortcut, but He chose not to. There was a very good reason for that:

> "Then it came to pass, when Pharaoh had let the people go, **that God did not lead them *by* way of the land of the Philistines, although that *was* near**; for God said, '**Lest perhaps the people change their minds when they see war, and return to Egypt**.'" (Exodus 13:17)

Taking the shortcut would have brought them to battles they were not ready to fight, which would have caused discouragement, doubt, and compromise. They would have turned and run back to Egypt. It was important in the mind of God that they go the long way around.

In wisdom and mercy, God took them that long way around. Might this be an answer to your question of, "Why is it taking me so long to get where I want to go?"

God knows and sees things we do not! He knows us better than we know ourselves! Without question, we can trust Him and His schedule for our lives.

We all think we know a faster route, a better way to do this, an easier way. But the journey prepares you for where you are and where you will be. It will always be the journey directed by God's hand that prepares you for your greatest success.

We are talking about your greatest success, and that comes when He is in control.

Here is a very serious question. Ask yourself:

Do I really want to control my own timing?

You may work hard. You aim. You try. And while these are all good, there must ultimately be a surrendering of your personal schedule to the King of Kings!

When you surrender all to the Father, you break the power of the enemy's plans. You spring the trap, and that slams shut the door of discouragement, so the enemy cannot enter through it.

Work hard, stay focused, and trust in God so that the pressure that leads to discouragement can no longer hang over your head.

That is trust in action, and that is a big part of walking free of discouragement.

So, *can* you really control your own timing? And even if you could, would you really *want* to?

Let God be God. Let Him direct your steps and you will come out ahead.

> "The steps of a good man are ordered by the Lord, and He delights in his way." (Psalm 37:23)

Handle the Delay

There have been times when I had trouble handling the delay. I was discouraged. I doubted I could do what I was called to do, if I had what it took, if I was doing the right thing.

Out of discouragement, I told God, "I quit."

I threw in the towel, only to have Him throw it right back at me!

He did not want me to quit. He does not want you to quit. He wants us to press forward. Let's let Him continue to do what He does best – to develop, chisel, shape, and mold us into His image.

Just because it's not happening right now does not mean it's not going to happen!

Yes, it may take far longer for something to happen than we think it should, but when it does finally happen, we will be ready for it!

It is so very vital that you remember a delay is not a denial. Daniel, in the Old Testament, certainly found that out.

> "The message was true, but the appointed time was long; and he understood the message, and had understanding of the vision." (Daniel 10:1-2)

When the appointed time is delayed, for whatever the reason, how will you respond?

Consider these strategies:

Refuse to compromise. The devil does not know your appointed time. He has no idea when the blessing is going to arrive. He just knows you are in pursuit and he wants to knock you out of the race before you get the prize. His goal is to get you to compromise. But if you will stay in the race, you will win in the end.

Keep pressing forward. Why quit one day too early? Every day you finish is one day closer to the manifestation of the blessing you are seeking. You are that much closer with each passing day.

Resist frustration. It is tempting to allow desires to turn into full-blown frustrations. For example, I have seen many single people get upset that they are not married yet. "God is too slow," they impatiently claim. "I'm running out of time." As a result of their frustrations, they go out and try to force the situation. It never ends well. Remember, delay is not denial.

Maintain the walk. Keep doing what you know is right, doing what you know you are called to do, and let the Lord handle the delay. After all, you really cannot do much about the timing anyway!

Keep a strong hold on your hope. Just because there is a delay does not mean God has forgotten about you or that the answer is a "No." Delay only means the time is not yet right. Keep your hope alive for all the good things He has planned for you.

Be ready, for if you press forward, trusting God, not giving up on your faith, it will happen. Your day will come!

God knows what you need and precisely when you need it.

And He will be there, right on time! You can count on that!

When was the last time you stopped and encouraged someone for no reason? Do it today!

Chapter Six

How to Overcome Discouragement

Discouragement must be dealt with on the most practical levels possible. The reality and serious impact of discouragement demand it. Fluffy words, clichés, or even best intentions will not be strong enough to overcome it.

Discouragement must always be dealt with before it deals with you.

Following are some tested and proven strategies that can be applied and put into use by you. Only then can you slam shut the door of discouragement in your life and keep it tightly closed.

If you battle discouragement and are committed to not compromising, these strategies will work for you:

Strategy #1: Resist

At the very first signs of discouragement, the believer must decide in his heart to resist it, realizing that it has no place in his life and making none available.

> "Therefore submit to God. Resist the devil and he will flee from you." (James 4:7)

To resist discouragement is to resist the offensive voice behind that discouragement, the devil. Head it off at the pass by resisting discouragement head on!

Strategy #2: Turn it over to the Lord

If you are struggling or worrying about your wants, needs, desires, etc., it basically means that you are not trusting God with it. This advice from scripture will help:

> "Commit your way to the Lord, trust also in Him, and He shall bring it to pass." (Psalm 37:5)

> "The Lord will perfect that which concerns me ...." (Psalm 138:8a)

> "... casting all your care upon Him, for He cares for you." (1 Peter 5:7)

Worry usually leads to discouragement. The more you struggle, the more struggles you have. The more you try to figure it out, the harder it becomes.

Instead, look up to Heaven. Turn it over to Him. He has a better way and He will give you wisdom as you seek Him and ask Him for it.

Rekindle your memories … that God is always faithful!

He will also anoint the wisdom you ask for when you simply trust Him for it.

So, give it all to Jesus.

Strategy #3: Remember past victories

The Jewish feasts were all celebrations in remembrance of Jehovah's provision, protection, and miracles. Similarly, you need to remember what God has done for you.

Hope can be dramatically rekindled when you say in your heart, "God, you did it back then for me. I know you will do it here again as well."

Sadly, we tend to forget so quickly what He has done for us. What happened to all the past victories? To remember is clearly to be encouraged. And, some people chalk up victories as their own – a direct result of their "self-made" efforts.

They forget the role that God played, but:

> "Every good gift and every perfect gift is from above, and comes down from the Father of Lights ...." (James 1:17a)

Remember, it was Him, not you, who made the victory possible. Reminding yourself of past victories in the Lord gives you great strength, hope, and peace.

Strategy #4: Keep a running file

Every single encouraging note, email, card, or verse I receive as a Pastor goes into my special "encouragement" file. Sometimes, if I'm feeling down and need encouragement, I simply flip open my "encouragement" file and see all those positive statements that are able to lift me up in no time.

> It is your responsibility to overcome.

They enable me to be patient, to keep at it, and to press on.

Truthfully, I have two files, one for encouraging words and another for discouraging words.

The first is a manila folder in my desk and the second is a round metal one beside my desk - and I empty it regularly!

Strategy #5: Choose your friends wisely

Only spend time with people who encourage and believe in you. They lift you up and love you for who you are. They do it just because!

Conversely, don't hang out with those "dead weights" - their negativity will suck the life and hope right out of you. They will always try to pull you back and keep you down.

Choose to spend time with people who love doing things God's way!

It will always be your best bet at remaining positive and successful!

Strategy #6: Encourage others

There is power in encouraging others. Even when you are feeling overwhelmed with your own worry, if you take a moment to encourage another person, it comes right back to you!

Feeling low? Go through your phone and send out a bunch of encouraging text messages. Send several emails. Doing so helps break the "funk" you are in.

This is actually the biblical principal of sowing and reaping in action. When you sow encouragement into others, you reap it right back into your life.

It is easy to do, and there will always be a positive return!

Strategy #7: Serve others

Just as encouraging others brings life back to you, so do purposeful acts of kindness done for others. It is the action behind your words and good intentions!

Serving others is a practical, sure way to get your mind off yourself. They need only be small acts of kindness that will minimally interrupt your day: mowing an elderly neighbor's lawn or washing his car are examples.

Of course, serving your pastor and your church family in a ministry will always be one of the most effective and rewarding ways to serve others because it is a service unto the Lord as well.

Your act of service is powerful and will help to break the grip of discouragement.

Strategy #8: Accomplish a goal

Every goal accomplished brings with it not only a good feeling but encouragement and a push to keep going forward.

While you are waiting for your big goal to be realized and find yourself battling discouragement, make a list of smaller, less dramatic things you want to do.

These are smaller goals that are attainable and don't require a massive amount of effort.

As you do those tasks and check them off the list, just the very accomplishment alone will bring you peace!

Yes, it is a small success, but it can pay you big "encouragement" dividends.

Strategy #9: Rest

We all need to rest. Comically, we drink coffee to wake up, drink more coffee to stay up, and then we complain that we cannot sleep at night.

When you are physically exhausted, it affects your emotions and your spirit. You may feel "down," but it could be that you are just tired. Go to bed early. Take a nap. Take a break. Taking care of yourself will rejuvenate you more than you know.

Strategy #10: Read the Word

The Word is full of encouragement. Consider some of these powerful Scriptures:

> "For whatever things were written before were written for our learning, that we through the patience and comfort of the Scriptures might have hope." (Romans 15:4)

> "And we know that all things work together for good to those who love God, to those who are the called according to *His* purpose." (Romans 8:28)

> "But thanks *be* to God, who gives us the victory through our Lord Jesus Christ." (1 Corinthians 15:57)

There are literally thousands of encouraging verses that will bring you hope when you need it most. Read the Word, pray the Word, speak the Word over yourself, and remind yourself of it regularly.

Strategy #11: Pray

No strategy could be more powerful and effective in overcoming discouragement than that of seeking God's advice, counsel, and guidance – through prayer.

He alone knows exactly what you need and the best way to go about getting those needs met. He alone knows what it will take to keep you encouraged and to keep you positive.

> Physical exhaustion opens the door for the enemy to neutralize you.

The Bible is filled with evidence of the "power of prayer."

Above all the strategies you might employ in overcoming discouragement, prayer and the Word should be, by far, your weapons of choice to use against the enemy when he comes to discourage you.

Because God has only your very best interests at heart, truly seeking His advice through earnest prayer and speaking the Word will always yield good results – building up both your physical and spirit man.

Meditate on prayer scriptures such as:

> "The effective, fervent prayer of a righteous man, avails much." (James 5:16b NKJV)
>
> "Be anxious for nothing, but in everything, by prayer and supplication, with thanksgiving, let your requests be made known to God." (Phil 4:6 NKJV)
>
> "So will my word be which goes out of my mouth; it will not return to Me void (useless, without result); without accomplishing what I desire, and without succeeding in the matter for which I sent it." (Isaiah 55:11 AMP)

Have frequent conversations with your Father. He longs to hear from you and He will never steer you wrong!

> Tell yourself the truth … over and over.

But be sure not to let your prayer become one-sided and speak or pray only the words you like hearing. They are often too few and too inadequate. Rather, be sure your prayers always include the Word of God.

Learn to speak the Word! Learn to pray the Word!

Strategy #12: Encourage yourself

Learn to speak words of faith and courage to yourself. Don't wait for others to see the need and offer to help. You have what it takes. Tell yourself the truth.

Everyone else saying good things about you could just be lip service.

It might be true, but you need to encourage yourself. You need to know that "you know that you know" the truth.

To tell yourself the truth may mean you need to do some homework - memorize scriptures, clarify your vision, or more.

Do not ask others to do this for you. It is your job and your responsibility.

Build your own self up! Stand on your own two feet! You can do it and you need to do it! It is your journey.

It rests on your shoulders and you must learn to encourage yourself.

Strategy #13: Get alone

Spend some time alone to disconnect from others, including your spouse, children, work, etc., so you can focus on just you and God. Breathe some fresh air. Get alone.

And when you are done, you will get back into it recharged, encouraged, and ready to go!

Strategy #14: Listen to trusted friends

Talking to a trusted friend can be helpful, but ONLY if that person is truly a trusted friend. It takes years to establish that type of friendship, so be very careful who you are listening to.

There is no room for gossip or judgment here. A trusted friend will listen and be the serious, solid, and trusted sounding board that you need.

> "As iron sharpens iron, so a man sharpens the countenance of his friend." (Proverbs 27:17 NKJV)

Strategy #15: Stir up the dream

Sometimes you need to go back and stir up the vision and dream you had when you first started.

As you know, anything worth having is worth fighting for, progressing toward, having faith for, and chasing after.

Yes, it will take effort, but it is well worth it in the end!

Your dream, vision, goal, and call are worth it. Press forward and let nothing keep you from achieving what is yours.

Remember, in God's eyes, you are "more than a conqueror," so be encouraged!

"Who satisfies your
mouth with good
things, so that your
youth is renewed
like the eagle's."
(Psalm 103:5)

CONCLUSION

I believe God is raising up people like you, dear reader, who are full of courage, faith, and potential – people who are focused on pursuing and hungry to experience the dreams and passions that God has created for them to enjoy.

I believe you understand that for all this to become a reality, you will need to be acutely aware of the tricks, schemes, ploys, and deceptions of the enemy.

To you the age-old traps of discouragement, doubt, and compromise are no longer a mystery. You will now know how they work, your guard is now always up, and you are keenly aware. And now you know what it will take to totally overcome them!

I pray you will let your life be what God wants it to be – a testimony for all to see of His goodness and blessing. Understand that He is watching over you affectionately and will not allow anything to overcome you.

Believe this, act on it, and do it with all your strength because it is His Will – it is true and it is for you!

No matter where you are and no matter what obstacles you are facing, keep pushing, pressing, and fighting forward until you break through. No matter how difficult, keep at it!

Never retreat, never quit, and never give in because your blessings and your heart's desires, with God's help, are on their way to you. They may be right around the next corner, so be encouraged, take heart, and press on.

You have been uniquely and wonderfully created to be more than a conqueror and always an overcomer!

"Delight yourself also
in the Lord, and He
shall give you the
desires of your heart."
(Psalm 37:4)

"… that if you confess
with your mouth that
Jesus Christ is Lord and
believe in your heart
that God has raised
Him from the dead,
you will
be saved."
(Romans 10:9)

YOUR PERSONAL PRAYER OF SALVATION

I trust that you have learned something meaningful from the principles I have outlined in *Discouragement, Doubt & Compromise.*

If you are a Born-Again believer, your knowledge of how best to overcome the 3-stage plan of the enemy will definitely help you to better live the prosperous, healthy and joyous life God the Father has created for you to enjoy.

If you are not a Born-Again believer, do not think that the devil will leave you alone. He wants to be sure that no one has the opportunity to serve God and he will do anything and everything to destroy you, Born-Again believer or not!

If you are not Born-Again and never received Jesus into your heart as your Lord and Savior – you need to do that right now!

In Romans 10: 9-10, the Bible says very clearly that *"If you say with your mouth that Jesus Christ is Lord and believe in your heart that God raised Him from the dead, you will be saved."*

Right where you are, right now, won't you please accept this wonderful gift of Salvation by lifting up your heart and saying aloud with your mouth, the following prayer:

> *Dear Jesus, I believe that you are the Son of God and that you died on the cross in payment for all of my sins.*
>
> *I also confess that the Father raised You from the dead and seated You forever more in Heaven at His Right Hand.*
>
> *I freely open the door to my heart and choose to make You the Lord of my life and my personal Savior. Right now, I repent of all my sins, receive your forgiveness and from this day forward, will live for you alone.*
>
> *Thank you, Lord Jesus, for loving me, forgiving me and saving my soul.*
>
> *Amen.*

If you sincerely prayed that prayer, you are now a Born-Again child of God, saved from hell and have just experienced the greatest miracle anyone could ever receive.

The Holy Spirit now lives in you and from this day forward, He will help you win every battle you will ever have to fight against the forces of evil in this world!

"I have come that they
may have life, and that
they may have it more
abundantly."
(John 10:10b)

MORE ABOUT THE AUTHOR

Raymond R. Hadjstylianos was born-again and filled with the Holy Spirit as a teenager by way of the Charismatic Movement of the 70's.

Fortunately, in those formative years when he could not find a local spirit-filled pastor to follow nor a caring church where he could be taught the uncompromised Word of God, he discovered the popular T.V. Ministry of Apostle Frederick K.C. Price, "Ever Increasing Faith," and his powerful Word of Faith message.

It was this television ministry on the far-off West Coast, that he necessarily followed, supported and recognized as his home church for years to come.

In the early 80's, his desire increasing to find a more local home church that professed a strong doctrine of faith; the born-again reliance on the Holy Spirit and; a message of the healing power of the Word of God, he jumped from denomination-to-denomination and church-to-church, but set down roots in none.

Finally, desperately looking for personal fellowship and a pastor he could submit to, he found a church to his liking and joined a local Assembly of God Fellowship.

His desire and willingness to serve being so evident, he was soon assigned to lead the Worship Team, mentor the Youth Group and conduct the Adult Bible Study.

After 3 years of faithful lay service, he was elevated to the position of Assistant Pastor in which he served in for the next 2 years.

Finally, he was awarded his Ministerial License and Certificate of Ordination in 1988 and feeling confident that God was leading him to organize his own ministry, incorporated as Living Word Christian Center: a congregation he pastored for the next 12 years.

In 1997, that congregation purchased land in White Plains, New York, on which now sits their modern, multi-million dollar church facility, which 1,500 + believers now call their home church.

In addition to his live weekend services, Pastor Ray has a growing, vibrant internet audience using today's most modern platforms of Live Stream, YouTube, Facebook and others, reaching increasing numbers of viewers across the U.S. and internationally.

He is also the Bible Study host and moderator of the Radio Outreach Ministry, "More Than Conquerors," currently on 18 radio stations, broadcasting weekdays across the nation to a potential listening audience of 35 million people.

Now, currently having preached the Gospel for more than 37 years, Pastor Ray continues to encourage with messages of faith that are alive, powerful and anointed, yet always presented in a personal and easily understood manner.

Weekly, he encourages his flock to live by faith; walk in integrity; and always seek a personal relationship with Jesus Christ–forever changing their lives and the lives of others they touch, as transformed by the Power of God!

www.PastorRayNY.com